Celebrate
Durga Puja With Me!

Shoumi Sen

Illustrated by Abira Das

ISBN-13:978-1517550073

ISBN-10:1517550076

To Riya, for all the joy you bring.
To Sanjeev, for everything.

Durga Puja marks the victory
Of good things over bad,
When Ma Durga defeated Mahisasur
And everyone was glad!

Heavens rejoiced amidst the sounds
Of conches far and near,
This great day of triumph
We celebrate every year!

As we start counting down
To this festival in the fall,
The days are filled with shopping sprees,
There's excitement at the mall!

Mahalaya marks the day
When Pujo is almost here,
We listen to tunes of the sacred hymn
That we've waited for all year!

The time has come, today is Shashti
And we finally get to see
Ma Durga and her children,
Ganesh, Kartik, Lakshmi and Saraswati.

Arati tonight is spectacular
With shiny lamps and dancing flames,
As we join together in prayer
To the goddess with 108 names!

We gather together for Anjali
There's scent of flowers in the air,
Listen to our wise purohit
As he leads us through the prayer.

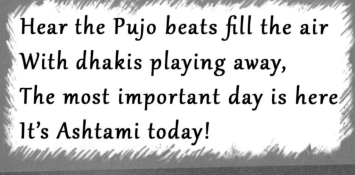

Hear the Pujo beats fill the air
With dhakis playing away,
The most important day is here
It's Ashtami today!

Navami evening is exciting,
Dhunuchi dancers perform their feats
Holding their smoky earthen bowls,
And dancing to the dhaki's beats!

And then it is Bisorjon,
Ma Durga is full of happy smiles
This now starts her journey home,
And she prepares to travel many miles...

To our elders we bow, friends we hug,
Wishing "Shubho Bijoya" to all
Asche bochor abar hobe,
We'll do this again next fall!

The End

About the Author

'From The Toddler Diaries' started as a series of poems that Shoumi wrote for her daughter. This collection, in its stapled makeshift binding, was the center of several bedtime story sessions and play dates with friends. Inspired by this interest amongst kids and encouraged by their parents, she decided to publish the collection.

Shoumi is a Strategy, Sales and Marketing professional at a leading Energy Management company. She grew up in Mumbai and Dubai and studied Engineering at BITS, Pilani and the University of Maryland, College Park. She loves to travel, has lived and worked in many countries, and currently lives in Los Angeles, California with her husband and daughter.

Visit Shoumi's website: www.shoumisen.com

About the Illustrator

From a very early age Abira was interested in the magical world of illustration and cartoons. She completed her graduation in Multimedia, Animation and Illustration from St. Xavier's College, Kolkata. She has worked on many books for authors from different countries and her illustrated books are available on Amazon.com.

Visit Abira's blog: www.abira-darkhues.blogspot.com

Made in the USA
San Bernardino, CA
15 September 2016